Thank you from the NSPCC

We would like to say thank you for taking part in the NSPCC Gherkin Challenge 2014 with this special edition of '*360 degrees at the Gherkin*'.

On average, it took participants 11 minutes to reach the top of the Gherkin. During that time, 33 children called *ChildLine* to help. The £200 you have raised will help pay for 50 calls to *ChildLine*. *(*A big thank you if you exceeded your target*)*.

When you look through this book and remind yourself of the views you saw, you can be confident in knowing that there are 50 children out there who now have somewhere to turn if they need support.

We hope you enjoy this book as a memento of your incredible achievement raising over £150,000 with the rest of the *Gherkin Challenge* team.
Every step you have taken will make a difference for children.

Cruelty to children must stop. FULL STOP.

360° at the Gherkin

A panoramic portrait by **Tee Dobinson**

Hi Jamie

8.19 – great job!

You're a star!

Tee D x

Design and art direction **Johnny Morris** - Original photography **Joe Plimmer**

New and old London
The Gherkin, completed in 2003 and the medieval church St Andrew Undershaft, a rare survivor of the Great Fire. Can you spot the workers on the dome installing the final panes of glass?

Welcome to this unique opportunity to view London in all its 360° glory. Foster + Partners designed 30 St Mary Axe, widely known as 'the Gherkin' and Lord Foster's vision for the space at the top delivers 'a chance to gain a sense of liberation from the streets.' In this guidebook there are eight panoramic photographs using the Gherkin as the centre of the compass and 100 places identified to help you translate the landscape. I have included conversation points for each location designed to inspire you to discover new places as well as delight in old favourites.

I use what I call the 'Gherkin Perspective' every day in my work. The view makes a great metaphor for the richness of life, we can see both the spectacular and the dilapidated laid out before us. The familiar stands alongside the unknown and there is always something fresh to consider and a host of new routes to discover. The vistas capture a series of moments in the continuing evolution of this great city, I hope you enjoy exploring them.

Tee Dobinson *The 'Gherkin Guru'*

Above *The stunning entrance of the Gherkin from the plaza.*
Right *The glass dome at the crown of the building.*
The bar at 'Searcys | The Gherkin' can be seen at the top with
the restaurant below on the 39th floor.

"From the earliest times men have sought to build high"

Norman Foster

"The most spectacular room in Europe"

Robin Partington

SOUTH

MID MORNING

8 Minster Court

4 City Hall

10 The Shard

3 Tower Bridge

5 All Hallows by the Tower

9 Hay's Galleria

6 Crystal Palace Transmitter

1 The Tower of London

HMS Belfast 7

Port of London Authority Building 2

The Willis Building

12 20 Fenchurch Street

13 The Lloyd's Building

Points
SOUTH

1 The Tower of London Although thousands of people were executed on Tower Hill only seven were executed inside on Tower Green. Six were beheaded with an axe but the seventh, Anne Boleyn, was allowed the swifter sword.

2 Port of London Authority Building Pevsner described this as 'a lasting monument to Edwardian optimism... showy, happily vulgar and extremely impressive.' Planning consent has been given to convert the building into a hotel.

3 Tower Bridge In 1953 Albert Gunter drove a double-decker red London bus with 20 passengers aboard across the central gap as the bridge was opening. The bus broke a spring, the conductor broke a leg, the driver and all passengers survived.

4 City Hall The geometrically modified spherical shape of this Foster + Partners building uses a quarter of the energy consumed by a typical high-specification office building.

5 All Hallows by the Tower Samuel Pepys climbed the red brick tower of this church to view the devastation caused by the 1666 Great Fire of London. The steeple covered in Zambian copper was added later.

6 Crystal Palace Transmitter Standing 219m high and sometimes referred to as Britain's Eiffel Tower. Television and radio signals have been broadcast from here since 1956.

7 HMS Belfast A floating branch of the Imperial War Museum. Its anchor weighs 5.5 tons, the same as an adult elephant.

8 Minster Court The inspiration for the current postmodern Gothic design was a convent that stood on the site 1,000 ago.

9 Hay's Galleria Originally an enclosed dock, Hay's Wharf, which received 80% of London's dry imported goods and was known as the 'Larder of London'.

10 The Shard Renzo Piano's 87-storey Shard is entirely encased in glass. At 306m it is currently the tallest building in Western Europe.

11 The Willis Building Foster + Partners' stepped roof design was intended to resemble the shell of a crustacean. Often you can spot people enjoying the view from the middle roof.

12 20 Fenchurch Street Christened the Walkie-Talkie for its distinctive shape, the top floors of the Rafael Viñoly design include a large viewing gallery and sky gardens.

13 The Lloyd's Building To maximise internal space the Richard Rogers Partnership put the lifts, toilets, refuse chutes, and air conditioning on the outside of the building along with piping for the electricity, wiring, drainage and plumbing.

SOUTHWEST

TWILIGHT

Cannon Street Station Tower 20

Shakespeare's Globe 23

Vauxhall Tower 17

The Monument 14

Battersea Power Station 18

Southwark Bridge 21

15 Golden Hind II

Tate Modern 22

16 Fishmongers' Hall

20 Gracechurch Street 19

NSPCC West London Service Centre

The Leadenhall Building

No. 1 Poultry

St Helen's

Points
SOUTHWEST

14 The Monument The distance from the base to where the Fire of London started is 202 feet, as is its height. The top was regilded with more than 30,000 gold leaves in 2009.

15 Golden Hind II A full-sized reconstruction of the ship Sir Francis Drake used to circumnavigate the globe between 1577-80, returning loaded with gold and silver.

16 Fishmongers' Hall Inside this livery company hall is the dagger with which Lord Mayor Walworth (a Fishmonger) killed Wat Tyler at Smithfield in 1381 during the Peasants' revolt.

17 Vauxhall Tower A wind turbine crowns the top of The St George's Tower (the building's official name). It is one of five planned towers for the Southern end of Vauxhall Bridge.

18 Battersea Power Station The deserted cathedral-like spaces and four white chimneys are to become a vibrant new community masterplanned by Rafael Viñoly Architects.

19 20 Gracechurch Street When this building was refurbished in 2004 the entrance was moved from Lombard Street to Gracechurch Street, creating a whole new address.

20 Cannon Street Station Tower In 1986 the Grade-II listed twin towers were restored and a large water tank used to fill steam locomotives was discovered in the east tower.

21 Southwark Bridge For 800 years Freemen of the City of London have had the inalienable right to drive sheep across Southwark Bridge and enter the City.

22 Tate Modern It cost £134m to convert the former Bankside Power Station into the Tate Modern. It has become the most visited modern art gallery in the world.

23 Shakespeare's Globe Sam Wanamaker persevered for over twenty years to get this built. It has the first and only thatched roof permitted in London since the 1666 Great Fire

24 St Helen's In the 1960s the 23-storey Commercial Union Building, at 118m, was the tallest in London.

25 The Leadenhall Building This new London icon is 224m high. The building's unusual shape, an ingenious solution by architects RSH+P to protect the view of St Paul's, has led to its nickname 'The Cheesegrater'.

26 No. 1 Poultry Before construction of this postmodern building the Museum of London excavated the remains of a wooden drain dating back to 47AD on the site, evidence of the founding of Roman London.

27 NSPCC West London Service Centre Here the NSPCC provide a number of vital services for children and parents including the safe reunification of children home from care.

Facing page *Helicopter shot revealing the geometry of the dome of the building.* **Clockwise from top left** *The Lloyd's Building lit up at night. The dome reflected in a glass of Leduc-Piedimonte Ice Cider Reserve. Late afternoon sunshine in the restaurant. The Gherkin viewed behind the Tower of London.*

Points
WEST

28 Green Park Royal 41 Gun Salutes are fired from here to mark the Queen's actual birthday (April 21st) and her official birthday (June 14th) as well as for the State Opening of Parliament and State Visits.

29 Blackfriars Railway Bridge Blackfriars Station, whose platforms now extend over the Thames, gets 50% of its power from 4,400 roof-mounted solar panels in the largest of only two solar bridges in the world.

30 The Royal Exchange Elizabeth I opened the first building here in 1571 and Queen Victoria opened this one, the third, in 1844. In 1669 stockbrokers were banned for being too noisy.

31 Unilever House A roof garden was added to this Grade-II listed Neo-classical Art Deco building with a tall curving frontage by Kohn Pederson Fox Associates.

32 The Bank of England There are three floors underneath the Bank and the bullion is kept in the middle one. You can't go into the vaults (hardly anyone ever gets this far) but you can handle a gold bar in the Bank of England museum.

33 St Mary le Bow The bells here rang the curfew in the 14th century. Each bell has a psalm engraved on it with the first letters spelling D WHITTINGTON, the three times mayor of London the bells famously made 'turn again'.

34 St Paul's Cathedral Sightlines to here are protected by eight view corridors from Alexandra Palace, Parliament Hill, Primrose Hill, Kenwood, Greenwich Park, Blackheath Point, Westminster Pier and King Henry's Mound in Richmond.

35 St Bride's The five-tiered steeple of this small Wren church behind Fleet Street has been used as the model for wedding cakes all over the world.

36 One New Change A series of terraces on the sixth floor provide a rare eye-level view of the dome of St Paul's Cathedral.

37 Former Stock Exchange This building was refurbished in 2008 rather than replaced, as it is now on a protected sightline and any new building on the site would have to be lower.

38 The Old Bailey This Central Criminal Court is named after the street on which it is located, which follows the line of the original fortified wall, or 'bailey', of the City.

39 The BT Tower This 177m high communications tower was protected by the Official Secrets Act and didn't appear on any maps until 1993, 30 years after construction.

40 Tower 42 183m high, with the three faces of Richard Seifert's hexagonal chevrons pointing to the traditional markets of Spitalfields, Old Billingsgate and Smithfield.

28 Green Park

The Bank of England

29 Blackfriars Railway Bridge

31 Unilever House

The Royal Exchange 30

WEST
EARLY EVENING

34 St Paul's Cathedral

39 The BT Tower

37 Former Stock Exchange

40 Tower 42

35 St Bride's

38 The Old Bailey

36 One New Change

33 St Mary le Bow

Points
NORTHWEST

41 Lauderdale, Barbican Tower One of the three towers in the Barbican complex, the others being Shakepeare and Cromwell. The 1960s development is a grade-II listed example of British brutalist architecture.

42 Moor House When it was built this Foster + Partners design had the deepest foundations in London, reaching down 57m to accommodate a Crossrail station below.

43 Crossrail Site Crossrail will run 118 km from Heathrow to Shenfield with 37 stations and eight sub-stations

44 The Barbican Arts Centre Europe's largest multi-arts and conference venue was built by the City of London Corporation and given as a gift to the nation in 1982.

45 Finsbury Circus The elliptical garden, listed gazebo and bowling green at the centre have been removed for the Crossrail work. Everything will be restored.

46 Pear Wood The Grim Dyke, Roman earthworks, cut across this high wood. Ancient plants under the trees include black bryony, hairy wood-rush and dog's mercury.

47 CityPoint In 2000 the former Britannic House was increased by 5m to 127m. A large fin that would have taken the height up to 203m was rejected.

48 Hampstead Heath Covering an area of 800 acres with three designated bathing ponds (Men's, Ladies' and Mixed) that have been in use for over a hundred years.

49 Primrose Hill 78m high, it offers outstanding views of the City, including a protected one of St Paul's. Kate Moss and Helena Bonham Carter are amongst the notable residents.

50 LSO St Luke's This former church with an unusual obelisk Hawksmoor spire is the home of the London Symphony Orchestra. The LSO has launched the YouTube Symphony Orchestra, the world's first-ever online orchestra.

51 St Pancras Station Art displayed here includes Martin Jenning's Betjeman Statue, a tribute to the poet who helped saved the station from demolition in the 1960s and the London 2012 Olympic rings, now recycled into station seats.

52 Liverpool Street Station Built on the site of the original Royal Bethlem psychiatric hospital, known as 'Bedlam' and notorious for its cruelty and inhumane treatment.

53 Alexandra Palace Named after Princess Alexandra the original palace was burnt down 16 days after completion but was immediately rebuilt. In 1936 the BBC broadcast the world's first regular television service from here.

The Barbican Arts Centre 44

Lauderdale, Barbican Tower 41

42 Moor House

43 Crossrail Site

NORTHWEST

48 Hampstead Heath

49 Primrose Hill

50 LSO St Luke's

Pear Wood

Alexandra Palace 53

51 St Pancras Station

47 CityPoint

Finsbury Circus

Liverpool Street Station 52

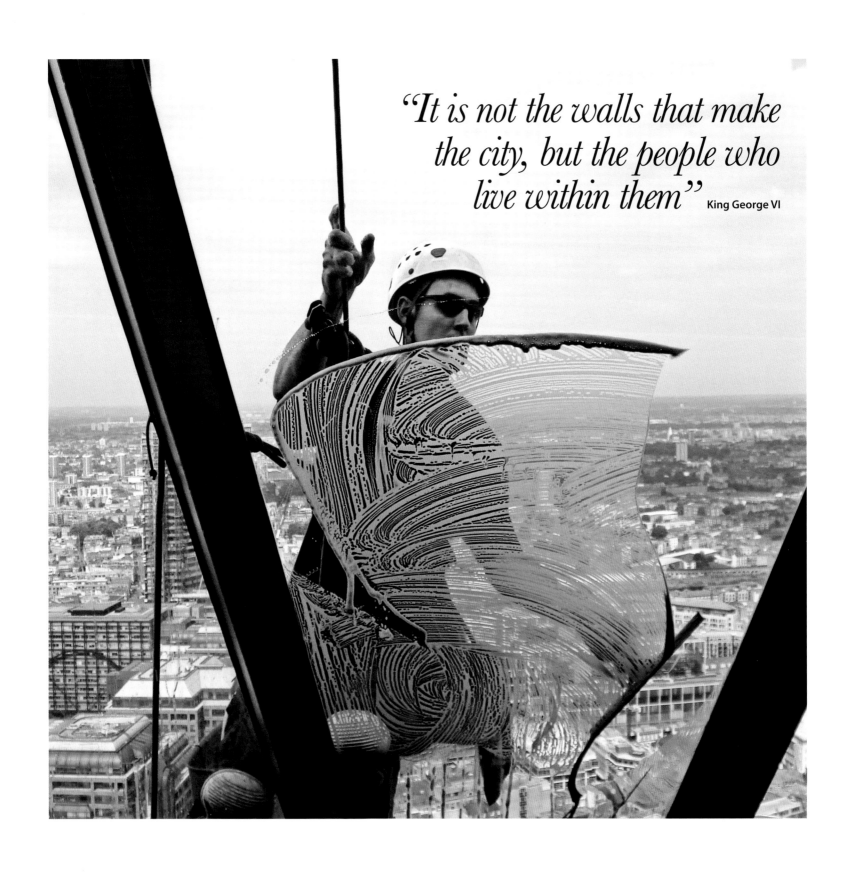

"It is not the walls that make the city, but the people who live within them" King George VI

Left *Window cleaner secured by a harness washing the glass of the dome. This is normally done using a cherrypicker.*
Clockwise from above *Looking northeast from the 'Searcys | The Gherkin' restaurant. Liverpool Street Station. Foie gras parfait, mandarin caramel, chestnut, pain poilâne.*

Points
NORTH

The Emirates Stadium 56

54 Finsbury Square

55 Alphabeta

54 Finsbury Square This is the oldest public park in London and the first place in the capital to have gas street lighting installed. A public bowling green opens here every summer.

55 Alphabeta A bronze figure of the Roman god Mercury by James Stephenson, originally exhibited at the Royal Academy, now stands on the summit of the former Triton Court.

56 The Emirates Stadium When Arsenal FC moved to the Emirates Stadium they brought the original clock that graced their former home for over 70 years with them. It sits high up on the outside facing the old 'clock end' of Highbury.

57 Heron Tower The tower is 202m tall, with the mast bringing it up to a height of 230m. The lobby features a 70,000 litre fish tank home to 1,200 fish.

58 Exchange House Looking out onto Exchange Square and Botero's five-ton bronze reclining nude *Venus*.

59 Broadgate Tower This is positioned directly over the lines into Liverpool Street station and, during construction, building had to stop every time a train went past.

60 155 Bishopsgate Part of the Broadgate Estate, 155 has a continuous frontage with 135 and 175 and its reception is host to two of Jim Dine's *Venus de Milo* inspired artworks.

61 Barings' Roof Terrace Phileas Fogg had his account at Barings Bank when he embarked upon his round-the-world journey. As he travelled east to west I like to imagine him looking out from this east-facing roof terrace before he set off.

62 The A10 This road starts on London Bridge, exits the city at Bishopsgate (one of seven gates in the wall around Roman London) and leaves London on the Roman route they named 'Ermine Street'. It ends in the Norfolk port of King's Lynn.

63 Shoreditch House London's East End branch of the fashionable members' club Soho House. A heated swimming pool is open all year round on the roof of this former factory.

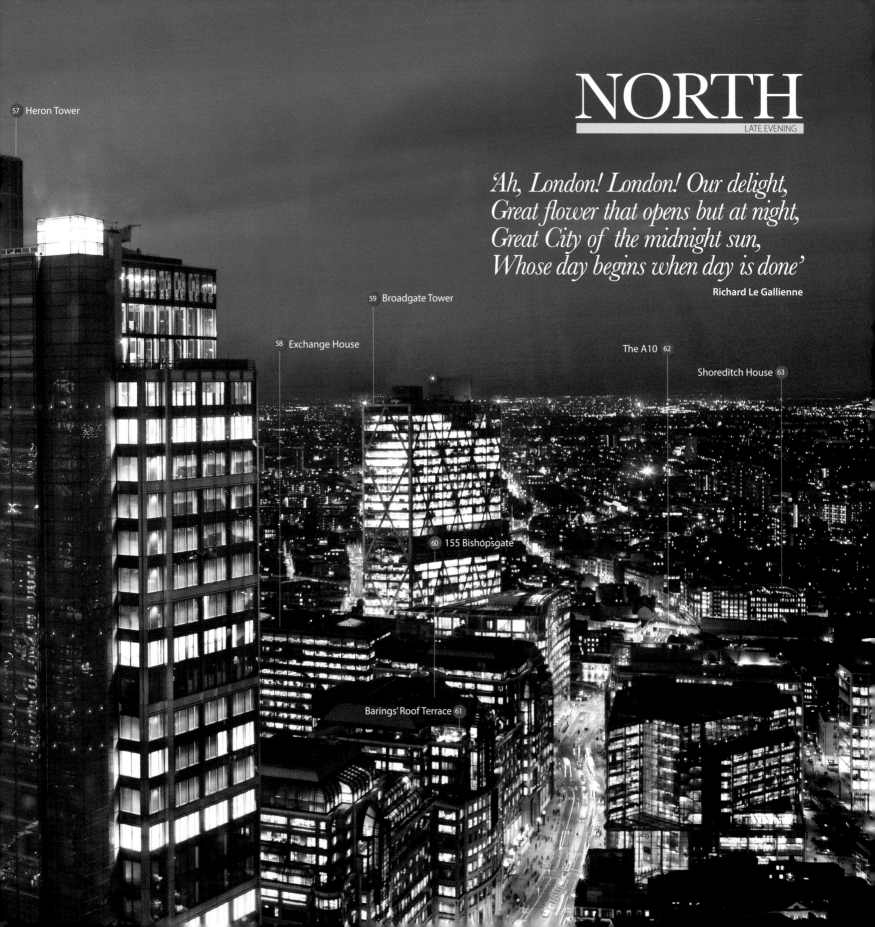

'Ah, London! London! Our delight,
Great flower that opens but at night,
Great City of the midnight sun,
Whose day begins when day is done'

Richard Le Gallienne

57 Heron Tower

59 Broadgate Tower

58 Exchange House

The A10 62

Shoreditch House 63

60 155 Bishopsgate

Barings' Roof Terrace 61

NORTH EAST
MIDDAY

70 The London Velodrome

65 Spitalfields Market

67 Truman Brewery Chimney

Weavers Field 69

64 One Bishops Square

68 Christchurch

66 Nido Spitalfields

The Olympic Stadium

The ArcelorMittal Orbit

Brick Lane

East London Mosque

Petticoat Lane Market

Beaufort House

64 One Bishops Square Allen & Overy's green roof includes solar panels and 580m of photovoltaic cells. In summer the red and purple umbrellas add vibrant colour to this Foster + Partners building.

65 Spitalfields Market The fruit and vegetable market that was here until 1991 dealt with produce from around the world with bananas being ripened in specially heated cellars.

66 Nido Spitalfields The tallest student accommodation in the world. Nido means nest in Spanish and Italian.

67 Truman Brewery Chimney The 49m high chimney with 'TRUMAN' displayed down its side overlooks an area of Brick Lane full of cultural venues and art galleries.

68 Christchurch Hawksmoor's masterpiece was successfully returned to glory in 2004. A dinner to honour local artists Gilbert and George was held here.

69 Weavers Fields Near the site of the biggest civilian disaster in World War II when 300 people were crushed in the stairwell of Bethnal Green tube station during an air raid. 173 died.

70 The London Velodrome Designed by Hopkins Architects, the GB Cycling Team won nine Olympic medals and 15 Paralympic medals here in 2012.

71 The Olympic Stadium The Opening and Closing Ceremonies of the London 2012 Olympic and Paralympic Games were held here along with the Athletics events.

72 The ArcelorMittal Orbit Created by sculptor Sir Anish Kapoor and designer Cecil Balmond, the looping structure stands 114.5m high in the Queen Elizabeth Olympic Park.

73 Brick Lane Named for the bricks and tiles manufactured here in the 16th century, the area is now famous for its Bangladeshi curries and as a centre of fashion and art. Street photographer Paul Trevor's Eastender Archive vividly captured this area in the 1970s and 80s.

74 Petticoat Lane Market Still named after the petticoats and lace sold there by French Huguenots, despite the Victorian local council's changing the street's name to Middlesex Street in an attempt to eradicate any reference to women's undergarments.

75 Beaufort House The 360° views change with the seasons. The deciduous trees that give us green vistas in summer disappear in the winter but the roof garden on this building remains an eye-catching emerald all year.

76 East London Mosque One of the largest mosques in Europe with space for 10,000 visitors at any one time.

Above *Aerial view of the Gherkin* **Right** *Looking at London having completed the NSPCC Gherkin Challenge* **Left** *Launch party of the 'Searcys | The Gherkin' Club* **Facing page** *The Club Lounge at sunset*

"So how can you tell me you're lonely,
And say for you that the sun don't shine?
Let me take you by the hand and lead you through the streets of London
I'll show you something to make you change your mind."

Ralph McTell

Points EAST

77 Royal London Hospital Helipad The London Air Ambulance operates 365 days a year, mobilises in under two minutes and can get a senior trauma doctor and a paramedic team to anywhere within the M25 in twelve minutes.

78 Whitechapel Bell Foundry The Olympic Bell for the London 2012 Olympic Games was designed here. Big Ben and the bells for the 2012 Queen's Diamond Jubilee Water Pageant were all cast on the premises.

79 London Metropolitan University The university started in 1848 as 'The Metropolitan Evening Classes for Young Men'.

80 The St Botolph Building Grimshaw Architects designed this characteristic blue banded building, its large central atrium is topped by a distinctive glass roof.

81 The Commercial Road This was built at the beginning of the 19th century by the East India Dock Company to accommodate traffic for the growing docklands.

82 Shadwell DLR Station The Docklands Light Railway opened here in 1987 with a platform for one-car trains. This was extended to accommodate two-car trains in 1991 and again for three-car trains in 2009.

83 St Botolph Aldgate One of the few City churches aligned north-south, instead of the usual east-west. The original church stood just outside the City walls at Aldgate and over 5,000 victims of the Plague were buried in its churchyard.

84 Queen Elizabeth II Bridge The white supports of this 137m high, 812m long cable-stay bridge at Dartford river crossing can be seen on a clear day.

85 One Canada Square When completed in 1991 this was, for one year, the tallest building in Europe. It remained the tallest building in the UK for ten years.

86 Canary Wharf Built on the former West India Docks the business area got its name from a warehouse that was used to store fruit from the Canary Islands. Jools Holland performed the first ever concert held here.

87 Sugar House The little clock tower on this Victorian former sugar warehouse is an exact quarter replica of Big Ben.

88 Shooters Hill Water Tower A Victorian Gothic tower built on one of the highest points in South London infamous as an area frequented by highwaymen. The singer Boy George used to live next door.

London Metropolitan University 79

77 Royal London Hospital Helipad

78 Whitechapel Bell Foundry

80 The St Botolph Building

EAST
SNOWY DAWN

81 The Commercial Road

82 Shadwell DLR Station

84 Queen Elizabeth II Bridge

85 One Canada Square

86 Canary Wharf

87 Sugar House

88 Shooters Hill Water Tower

83 St Botolph Aldgate

Points
SOUTHEAST

89 London City Airport Using 'short take off and landing' planes the airport is situated between the King George V and Royal Albert Docks.

90 The O2 (formerly the Millennium Dome) The white exterior has twelve 100m high yellow support towers, one for each month of the year or for each hour of the clock face and there are 365 arcs on the edges of the dome, one for each day of the year. All designed to honour Greenwich Mean Time.

91 Rotherhithe Tunnel Completed in 1908, its curves were to prevent the horses from bolting towards the light at the end of the tunnel. You can still see the bases of the spiral staircases for pedestrians from the old riverside shafts as you drive through.

92 Latham House This 1980s Minories office block has been empty and scheduled for demolition since 2007 with planning permission granted for Trinity.EC3, three glazed buildings resembling a cluster of crystals.

93 Shadwell Basin The most easterly part of the former London Docks and one of the few areas that has not been land-filled. It is now used for sailing, canoeing and fishing.

94 Grange Tower Bridge Hotel Built over a part of the East London Roman Cemetery unexcavated until 1984, a rare circular mirror box and a pendant, both with Nero's head on and dating from 67- 68 AD, were found in a cremation jar.

95 Old Royal Naval College Arguably the finest example of Baroque architecture in the UK and featuring in many films including *Four Weddings and A Funeral, The King's Speech, Sherlock Holmes, Les Miserables* and *Muppets Most Wanted.*

96 The Royal Observatory Home of Greenwich Mean Time, the Harrison timekeepers, the UK's largest refracting telescope and the Prime Meridian of the World, Longitude 0°.

97 St Thomas More Square News International Ltd moved into number 3 here in 2009. Two years earlier they had become the UK's first carbon neutral newspaper publisher.

98 St Katherine's Dock Formerly a dock handling rum, brandy, sugar, spices, perfumes, ivory, marble, shells and tea and now a marina for luxury yachts.

99 SELCHP The South East London Combined Heat & Power Energy Recovery Centre uses 420,000 tonnes of waste from London homes and businesses annually to produce electricity to power 48,000 homes.

100 The Den Millwall FC's sixth ground. The club were based north of the river for 24 years before moving their home to south of the river in 1910.

89 London City Airport

90 The O2

91 Rotherhithe Tunnel

93 Shadwell Basin

92 Latham House

SOUTHEAST

LATE AFTERNOON

95 Old Royal Naval College

94 Grange Tower Bridge Hotel

96 The Royal Observatory

SELCHP 99

The Den 100

97 St Thomas More Square

98 St Katherine's Dock

"If you're tired of London, you're tired of life" Samuel Johnson

Above *Drinks in the 'Searcys | The Gherkin' bar overlooking the city at night*

GHERKIN BY NUMBERS

24,000 square metres of external glass cover the building, equivalent to **5** football pitches.

70,000 tons is the weight of the building fully occupied.

4,000 people can work in the **33** floors of offices in the building.

The year the original owners, Swiss Re, began moving into their new headquarters was **2003**

378 people can be simultaneously transported up the building in the **18** lifts.

299 events are held at the top every year.

180 metres is the height of the building, making it more than **3** times higher than Niagara Falls.

2014 - the **10th** anniversary of the official opening of the building.

40 floors - the very top one being the bar in the dome where you can experience **360°** views across London.

35 kilometres of structural steel weighing **11,000** tons were used in the construction process.

30 St Mary Axe is both the building's address and its official name.

21 couples have their weddings at the top of the Gherkin every year.

16th this is the widest floor, with a circumference of only **2** metres less than the height of the building.

11 prestigious architectural awards won including the RIBA Stirling Prize.

6 metres per second is the speed of the high-rise lift (and yes, your ears do pop!)

5 degrees is the amount each floor rotates from the one below.

4 minutes and **18** seconds is the time it took record holder Matthias Jahn to run up the stairs to the **38th** floor in the

NSPCC's annual Gherkin Challenge event (amazingly that's almost faster than the super-fast lifts).

1 piece of curved glass, which is the lens at the very top of the building.

360° at the Gherkin

A PROPOSAL TO REMEMBER

Emma Ticehurst, who features on our cover and opposite in a red coat, will remember her visit to the top of the Gherkin for a very special reason. In the Club Lounge at the end of the evening, with London glittering in front of them, her partner Ben asked her to marry him. Emma said yes.

THANKS TO

Kent Gardner of Evans Randall for his time and encouragement.
Danny Kaljee, Sarah McQueen, Karim LeCloarec and Joel Claustre at Searcys for their continued support.
Antonio, Kenan, Naeem, Rene, Zerin, Jess and Neil Burton for kindly agreeing to appear in our photographs.
Carolyn Webb, City of London Tour Guide and Dan Ash, Building Surveyor and Conservationist, for excellent research and for being a pleasure to work with.
Johnny Morris for his creative genius and Joe Plimmer for his exquisite photography.
Sara Fox, Swiss Re Project Director, for being so generous with her time and expertise.
Lorraine Sage of Swiss Re for lunch.
PremiAir for their help with the aerial shot of the Gherkin.

BIBLIOGRAPHY

30 St Mary Axe A Tower for London – Kenneth Powell - Merrell
Five Hundred Buildings of London – John Reynolds & Gill Davies – Black Dog & Leventhal Publishers
London from the Thames – Angelo Hornak – Little, Brown and Company
Norman Foster A life in Architecture – Deyan Sudjic – Orion Books
Spectacular Venacular – David Long - Sutton Publishing
The London Encyclopaedia – Edited by Ben Weinreb, Christopher Hibbert, Julia Keay, John Keay – Macmillan
The Visitor's Guide to the City of London Churches – Tony Tucker – The Friends of the City Churches
Walking London – Andrew Duncan - New Holland Publishers

WEB

30stmaryaxe.com
cityoflondon.gov.uk
fosterandpartners.com
london.gov.uk
lparchaeology.com
skyscrapernews.com
london.lovesguide.com

MAPS

Ordnance Survey Maps: 162 - Greenwich & Gravesend 173 - London North 161 - London South
The City of London Map 2008-9 - in conjunction with the City of London *Premier Map of London* - A-Z publication Edition 9

CREDITS

Art direction and design - **Johnny Morris** baizdon.com
Concept and text **Tee Dobinson** teedobinson.com

Photo of the Gherkin in 2003 Nigel Young, Foster + Partners NSPCC Gherkin Challenge Sam Mellish
Additional photographs - courtesy of Searcys

CONTACTS

Searcys | The Gherkin Enquiries **020 7071 5025** Membership **020 7071 7215** Events **020 7071 5009** searcys.co.uk/the-gherkin
Gherkin Talks Tee Dobinson **07966 190712**